A Practical Guide for

Developing Management

Information System for NGOs

Vamathevan Valavan

Consultant

TT HOMES

ABOUT THIS GUIDEBOOK

Data has become fundamental in nearly every aspect of life. With the growing importance placed on data, managing data has become a central focus for every organisation, from billion-dollar tech companies to rural non-profits - this user-friendly guidebook targets primarily non-profit organisations.

Effective information management is crucial to successful programme implementation. Having worked for more than ten years as a Monitoring, Evaluation, Accountability and Learning (MEAL) professional, I have noticed many (but not all) professionals working in non-profit organisations have faced difficulties in handling data because they miss the fundamental principle: not everything that counts can be counted, and not everything that can be counted counts. To overcome this, one should have a clear idea of what types of information are needed to make which decisions, which determines what data needs to be collected.

There is no magic formula for setting up a Management Information System (MIS) as it is an individually designed system that requires thorough needs analysis and specialised development. However, this guidebook approaches this concept from a different point of view. It lessens the complexity of developing an effective MIS, as well as explains how MIS works from planning through to the dissemination stage.

This guidebook takes readers through two parts. Part 1 of this guidebook describes the basic concepts of the MIS in "question and answer" form, whereas Part 2 explains the key steps involved in developing an MIS. The information is presented in a concise, direct-to-the-point, easy-reading format.

I look forward to receiving your feedback, so we can further improve what has been provided here.

V. Valavan
Consultant
Mail: vlavan14@gmail.com

TABLE OF CONTENTS

1 MANAGEMENT INFORMATION SYSTEM (MIS)   5
    1.1: Why is information management so important?   5
    1.2: What is MIS?   5
    1.3: What are the types of MIS commonly used?   5
    1.4: What are the key elements of MIS?   6
    1.5: What are the differences between data and information?   6
    1.6: What are the different data types and commonly referenced key aspects of data quality?   7
    1.7: What type of information does MIS provide?   8
    1.8: Who needs what information?   9
    1.9: How does MIS help NGOs?   13
    1.10: How does MIS work?   14
    1.11: How does MIS feed into M&E?   15
    1.12: What are the key stages involved in developing an MIS?   16

2 DEVELOPING A MANAGEMENT INFORMATION SYSTEM (MIS)   17
    2.1: Stage 1 - Determine actors, their roles, and the types of information they need   17
        Step 1: List the actors connected with the social fund   17
        Step 2: Identify the key functions/roles of the actors connected with the social fund   18
        Step 3: Decide what types of information actors need   20
    2.2: Stage 2 - Data management   23
        Step 1: Define data needs   24
        Step 2: Determining the information and data flow   29
        Step 3: Planning data collection   31

Step 4: Data analysis 36
Step 5: Ensuring data security 46
2.3 Stage 3: Dissemination of data and information 47

ANNEX 1 49

1 MANAGEMENT INFORMATION SYSTEM (MIS)

1.1: Why is information management so important?

- It provides information support to the decision-making process at each level of an organisation.
- It assists organisations to better plan, manage and coordinate their programmes.
- It assists in exchanging related information (e.g., status of the population served), experiences, expertise and learning resources.
- It assists in demonstrating to a broader audience how the organisation works.

1.2: What is MIS?

A management information system is an organised information and documentation service that systematically collects, stores, processes, analyses, interprets, and disseminates data and information in an organised manner to guide management decisions and provide a broad picture of the services to programme renders and other relevant stakeholders (governments, communities, end-users, etc.) at the right time.

1.3: What are the types of MIS commonly used?

- Computerised MIS
- Semi-computerised MIS (using MS Office packages, statistical packages, etc.)
- Manual MIS

In most cases, NGOs prefer to adopt semi-computerised MIS as it is easy to manage and less expensive.

1.4: What are the key elements of MIS?

A. **Actors** - who use the information (produced by the programme/project) to take decisions that directly or indirectly affect the programme/project or its environment.
B. **Data** and **information** – that is useful for decision-making.
C. **Procedures** - that determine how the actors relate to the data.
D. **Tools** - facilitate the collection, analysis, storage and dissemination of the data and information.

1.5: What are the differences between data and information?

Data[1] is an unsystematic fact (raw fact) or detail about something or someone, whereas information is a systematic and filtered form of data which is useful.

When the data is transformed into information, it is free from unnecessary details or immaterial things, so it has some value to the users.

Comparison between data and information

Table 1

Basis for comparison	Data	Information
What is it?	It is just text, numbers, figures, symbols, simple description of things/events	It is refined data. Free from unnecessary details or immaterial things. It has some value to the user
Based on	Records and observations	Analysis
Form	Unorganised or unsystematic	Organised or systematic

---

[1] Data is bare and random

Useful	May or may not be useful	Always useful
Specific	No	Yes
Dependency	Does not depend on information	Without data, information cannot be processed
Example	Test score of a particular subject of a student is one piece of data	The average score of a class in a particular subject is information that can be derived from the given data

1.6: What are the data types and commonly referenced key aspects of data quality?

There can be two types of data:
- Primary Data
    - Qualitative Data
    - Quantitative Data

- Secondary Data
    - Internal Data (qualitative and quantitative)
    - External Data (qualitative and quantitative)

Commonly referenced key aspects of data quality

- **Validity:** Data measures what it is intended to measure.
- **Reliability:** Data is measured and collected consistently according to standard definitions and methodologies; the results are the same when measurements are repeated.
- **Accuracy:** How close the measurement taken is to the actual (true) value.
- **Completeness:** All data elements are included (per the specified definitions and methodologies).

- **Precision[2]:** Data has sufficient detail (in a social context)
- **Integrity:** Data is protected from deliberate bias or manipulation for political or personal reasons.
- **Timeliness:** Data is up to date (current), and information is available on time.

1.7: What type of information does MIS provide?

A well-designed MIS provides vital and up-to-date operational, functional and performance information.

Operational Information

This information reveals:

- how the project functions vis-a-vis outputs, schedules, and use of resources; and
- faced constraints, risks and positive changes along the way

> Operational Information = Output + Process of the output + Challenges, constraints and positive aspects along the way.

Functional information (organisation related)

Functional level information indicates:

- how well programme, finance, logistics and HR units/departments work together;
- ongoing needs of the organisation;
- status of the physical assets (stock, vehicle movements & maintenance, working condition of the equipment, etc.); and

---

[2] Precision (scientific context) - precision is the degree to which repeated measurements under unchanged conditions show the same results.

- staff-related matters (knowledge, attitudes, skills, performance, salary, etc.).

Performance Information

Performance information assists in assessing:

- how well an organisation is meeting its objectives (effectiveness[3], efficiency[4], relevance[5]);
- effects of the intervention (impact[6]) on end users (beneficiaries or communities);
- continued long-term benefits (sustainability[7]); and
- the reasons for the results (changes).

1.8: Who needs what information[8]?

Before developing an MIS, it is essential to identify the following:

- Who uses what information to make what type of decision?
- Who will provide this information?

---

[3] The extent to which the development intervention's objectives were achieved, or are expected to be achieved, taking into account their relative importance.

[4] A measure of how economically resources/inputs (funds, expertise, time, etc.) are converted to results.

[5] The extent to which the objectives of a development intervention are consistent with beneficiaries' requirements, country needs, global priorities and partners' and donors' policies.

[6] Positive and negative, primary and secondary long-term effects produced by a development intervention, directly or indirectly, intended or unintended.

[7] The continuation of benefits from a development intervention after major development assistance has been completed. The probability of continued long-term benefits. The resilience to risk of the net benefit flows over time.

[8] Adapted from *De MIStifying M I S: Guidelines for Management Information Systems in Social Funds*.

The response to this question will differ for each project and require special attention in each case. There are commonly four main actors involved in the social fund (programme/projects).

- Social fund personnel
- Social fund management
- Government
- Donors

Social fund personnel

The daily work of the NGO generates (and is supported by) large amounts of detailed operational data, which are collected throughout the lifetime of each project. These are:

- Details of the beneficiaries (their socio-economic status, location, age, gender, living environment, type of service received, etc.).
- Details of the contractors, service providers and intermediaries (their addresses, areas of operation, references, etc.).
- Data related to financial management and accounting (budgets, commitments, and disbursements).
- Technical data on each project, its progress (sector/sub-sector, technical characteristics, performance indicators), and contractual obligations.

In addition to this, the day-to-day operation requires data on its internal functioning, such as:

- Human resources (organogram, the composition of various units, leave schedule, personnel evaluations, etc.)
- Physical assets (supply stocks, vehicle movements and maintenance, working condition of the equipment, etc.)
- Overall financial management (budgets, commitments and disbursements, spent amount, etc.)

This operational data allows the social fund personnel to take decisions and guide their day-to-day activities (decisions regarding field visits, meeting deadlines, equipment status, etc.). Processed operational data assists management decision-making.

Social fund Management

The management body of the NGO must take decisions on the following major areas in which information needs tend to be clearly defined:

- Local needs (socio-economic profile of beneficiaries, geographic location and sector of proposed intervention) and ongoing and completed activities.

- Key challenges (external and internal), risks faced during implementation, what works well and what does not, etc.

- Effectiveness (are the desired results being achieved as per the plan?), efficiency (are we using the available resources appropriately?), relevance (does the project address current needs?), impact (have the objectives/goal been achieved? What changes have occurred that help beneficiaries?) and sustainability (will the impact be sustainable?)

- Internal performance of the agency's different parts (departments/units) (functional level information - logistics, finance, HR related, working condition, working condition of equipment, etc.)

The above information assists the management body:
- to ensure smooth implementation of the planned interventions – to better plan, manage and coordinate its programme; and
- to focus on future interventions, strategies and the organisation's policy.

Government

The main functions of the Government in social funds are:

- a control function; and

- strategic or policy function.

It, therefore, requires two types of information:

- for its control function, it needs access to financial, accounting and procurement information; and
- for its strategic function (the social fund generally being part of a broader anti-poverty strategy), it needs to know the impact of social fund activities broken down by categories such as location, sector, beneficiary group and year/month.

Donors

Donor information needs are similar to government information: detailed information to monitor procurement and disbursement and aggregate information to measure impact.

Note: Government and donors request the NGOs provide information in standard formats (circulated by the government/donors) that capture the required information (control and policy).

Figure 1 summarises the information needs of the different actors.

Figure 1 - Information Needs in a Social Fund

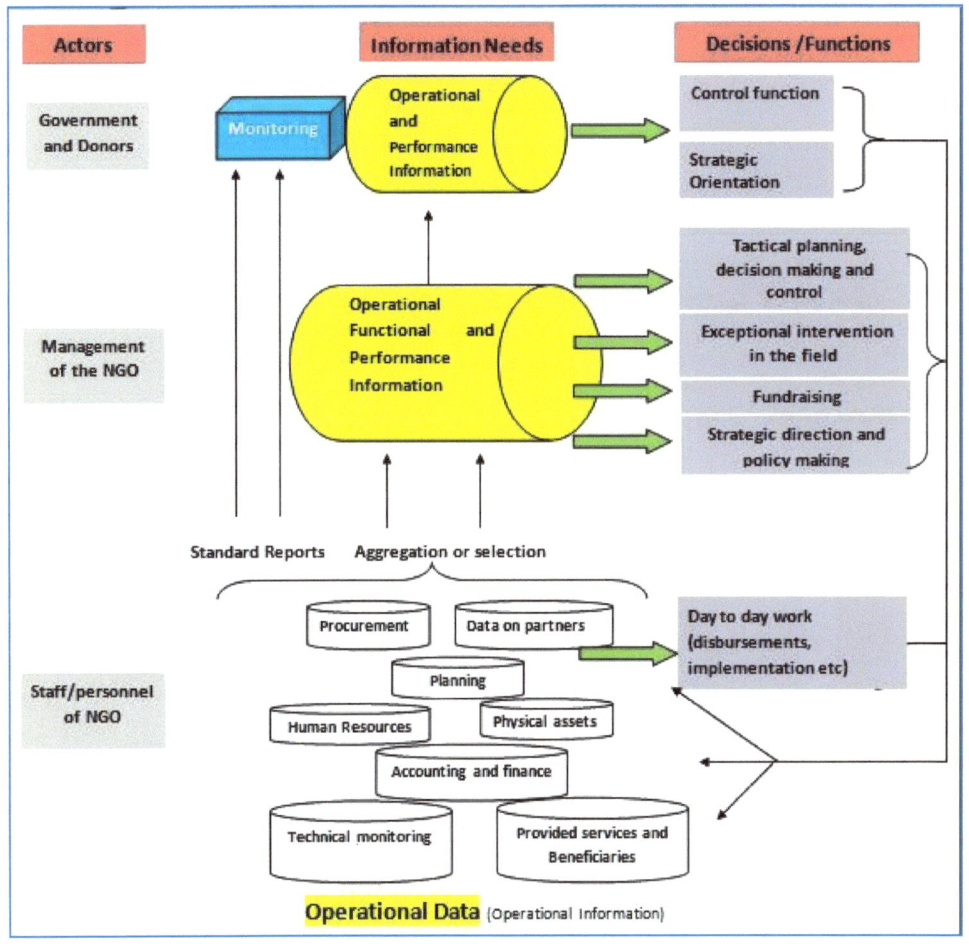

1.9: How does MIS help NGOs?

An MIS assists to:

- identify problems and find solutions;

- evaluate the impact of programmes;
- better utilise resources;
- identify implementation tactics;
- monitor programme activities;
- plan and coordinate programme activities;
- develop long-term strategies;
- provide information on the status of the population served;
- guide in choosing entry points for programme interventions and establish active partnerships with other organisations; and
- forecast commodity or service needs, service delivery constraints, and improvement methods.

1.10: How does MIS work?

Figure 2:

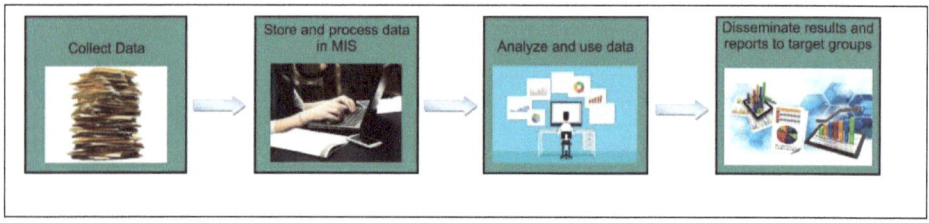

1.11: How does MIS feed into M&E?

Figure 3 illustrates how monitoring and evaluation converge are interdependent, in what ways they are separate, and how an MIS fuels both activities.

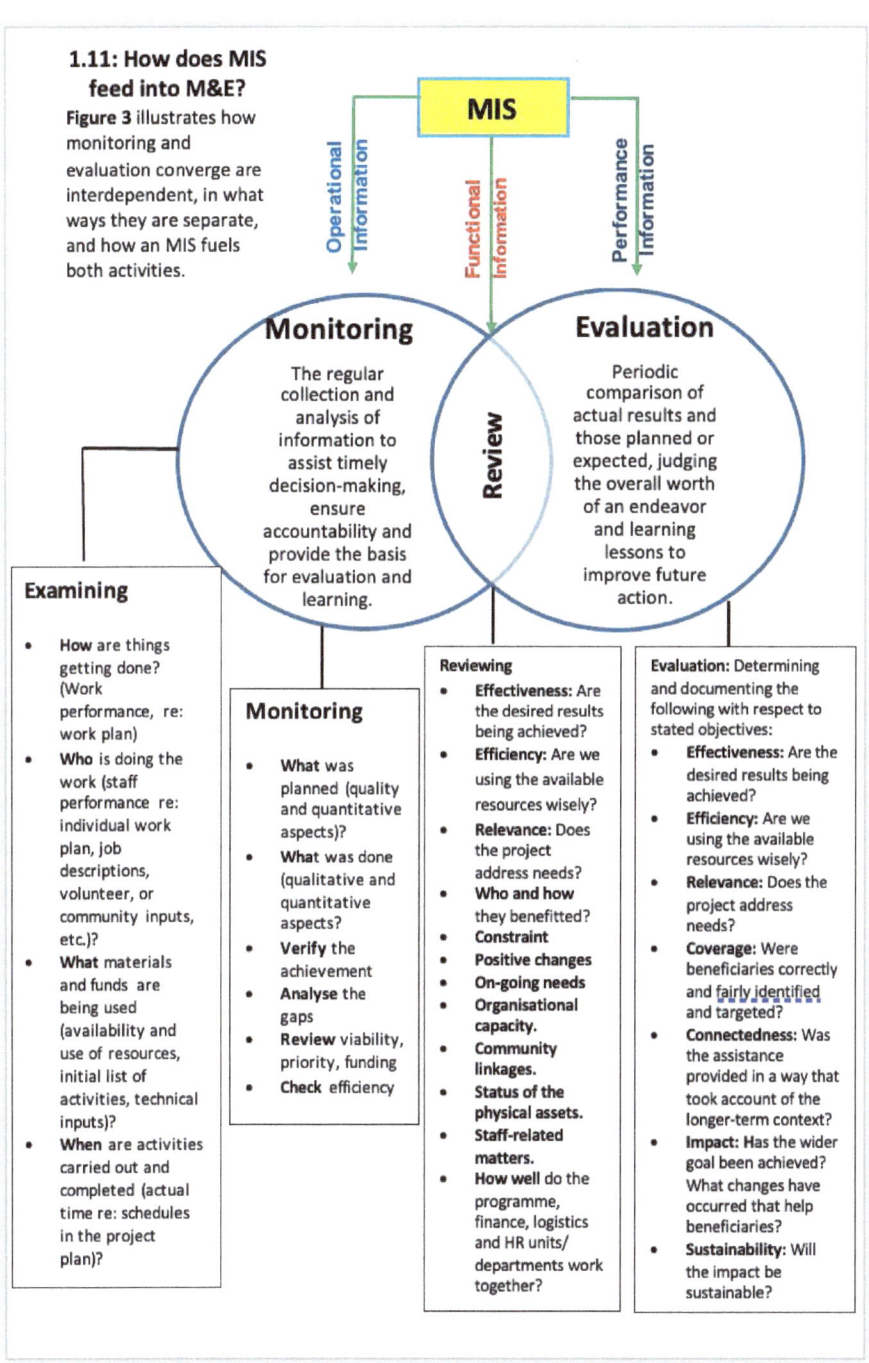

1.12: What are the key stages involved in developing an MIS?

The step-by-step approach is explained in section 2 of this guidebook.

2 DEVELOPING MANAGEMENT INFORMATION SYSTEMS (MIS)

2.1: Stage 1: Determine actors, their roles, and the types of information they need

Keynotes

1. To create an effective MIS, the developer needs to clearly understand the actors involved in the social fund (programme/project).
2. Different actors in the social fund (internal and external) have different roles and therefore have different data needs.
3. Not everything that counts can be counted, and not everything that can be counted counts.

Suggested questions to identify key players in a social fund

- Who uses the information to make what decisions?
- Who will provide this information?

The response to these questions will differ for each project and requires special attention in each case.

Step 1: List the actors connected with the social fund.

The following actors (internal and external) are involved in a social fund:

- Project team;
- Management body of the organisation (decision-making authority, executive committee, etc.);
- Donors;
- Government (all government stakeholders);
- Partners;
- End-users (target group);

- Other stakeholders[9] - (other NGOs, community-based organisations, community leaders, vendors, etc.).

Step 2: Identify the key functions/roles of the actors connected with the social fund

Table 2

Actors	Essential Functions/role related social fund
Programme/project team	Operation • Successfully implement the programme/project (plan, implement, monitor, evaluate, document, report, etc.) • Support the M&E team in generating information

Management body	1. Management function (operational and functional)
	• Tactical planning, decision-making and control to:
	   ○ provide required guidance to the programme/project team; and
	   ○ ensure effective internal performance of the different sections of the organisation.
	2. Strategic function
	• Fund-raising (winning projects, generating own funds, etc.)
	• Providing strategic direction and policy-making decisions at an organisational level

---

[9] These stakeholders are those who can influence the programme/projects or will be affected either positively or negatively.

Donors	- Control function. - Strategic or policy function
Government	- Control function - Strategic or policy function
Partners	It depends on the partnership agreement (institutional or programme/project partnership). The function of the partners is similar to the programme/project team and management body
End users (target group)	Contribute and support the programme/ project team to successfully implement the programme/project. **Note:** - End-users are part of the social fund (programme/project). - Engagement of the target groups (in the programme/project cycle) is crucial to programme/project success. - Therefore, the programme/project team's responsibility is to ensure that target groups receive the right kind of information at the right time, and their views must be carefully analysed and incorporated into the operational plan.

Other stakeholders[10]	• These are stakeholders who are not directly connected to the decision-making loop of the social fund (programme/project). **Note:** • Even though they are not directly connected to the decision-making loop, they can affect the programme/project positively or negatively. • Due attention should be paid to manage them effectively without negatively impacting the programme/project with minimum effort and resources.

Step 3: Decide what types of information actors need

There are three types of information which must be in place for effective programme/project management (see section 1.7):

- Operational information
- Functional information
- Performance information

For further details, please see Table 3.

---

[10] These stakeholders are those who can influence the programme/projects or will be affected either positively or negatively.

Table 3

Actors	Essential Functions/role related social fund	Types of information they need
Programme/project team	<u>Operation</u> • Successfully implement the programme/projects (plan, implement, monitor, evaluate, document, report etc.) • Support the M&E team in generating information	Operational information

Management body	<u>Management function</u>
	• Tactical planning, decision-making and control
	   ○ providing required guidance to the programme/project team
	   ○ ensuring effective internal performance of the different sections of the organisation
	
	<u>Strategic function</u>
	• Fund-raising (winning projects, generating own funding, etc.)
	• Providing strategic direction and policy-making decisions at an organisational level
		<u>Management function</u>
		• Operational information
		• Functional information
		
		<u>Strategic function</u>
		• Performance information

Donors	• Control function • Strategic or policy function	<u>Control function</u> • Operational information (procurements details,

		accounting information, process information, etc.) Strategic function • Performance information
Government	• Control function • Strategic or policy function	Similar to donor
Partners	It depends on the partnership agreement (institutional or programme/ project partnership). The function of the partners is similar to that of the programme/project team and management body	Either operational or performance information or both (depending on the partnership agreement)
End-users (target group)	Contribute and support the programme/ project team for the successful implementation of the project. **Note:** • End-users are part of the social fund (programme/project) • Engagement of the target groups (in the programme/project cycle) is crucial to programme/project success • Therefore, the project team's responsibility is to ensure that target groups receive the right kind of information at the right time, and their views must be carefully analysed and	Both operational and performance information

	incorporated into the operational plan	
Other stakeholders	- These are stakeholders who are not directly connected to the decision-making loop of the social fund (programme/project). **Note:** - Even though they are not directly connected to the decision-making loop, they can positively or negatively affect the programme/project. - Due attention should be paid to managing other stakeholders effectively without negatively impacting the project, with minimum effort and resources.	Operational and performance information (depending on the needs and circumstances)

2.2: Stage 2 - Data management

Remember
Good data management includes developing effective processes for consistently collecting and recording data, storing data securely, cleaning data, transferring data (e.g., between different types of software used for analysis), effectively presenting data and making data accessible for verification and use by others.

Commonly referred to aspects of data quality are:
- **Validity:** Data measures what it is intended to measure.
- **Reliability:** Data is measured and collected consistently according to standard definitions and methodologies; the results are the same when measurements are repeated.

> - **Completeness:** All data elements are included (per the specified definitions and methodologies).
> - **Precision:** Data has sufficient detail[11].
> - **Integrity:** Data is protected from deliberate bias or manipulation for political or personal reasons.
> - **Timeliness:** Data is up-to-date (current), and information is available on time.
>
> Adapted from *Overview: Data Collection and Analysis Methods in Impact Evaluation (Methodological Briefs Impact Evaluation No. 10 UNICEF)*

Step 1: Define the data needs

As mentioned in step 3 of stage 1 (page 16), there are three types of information which must be in place for effective programme/project management:

- Operational information
- Functional information
- Performance information

We cannot collect all necessary data for reasons such as time constraints, restrictions, expenses, etc. Therefore, attention should be paid to collecting data describing what we seek at the operational, functional and performance levels.

<u>At operational level</u>

The following information should be in place for successful operation.

- Information related to process - whether activities are implemented per the plan and set standards [time frame, budget, sequence order, in line

---

[11] A more specific definition for quantitative measurements is as follows: a measurement is considered 'valid' if it is both 'accurate' and 'precise'. Accuracy is defined as the deviation from the 'true' value and precision is defined as the 'scatter'. In other words, accuracy is about how close the measurement taken is to the actual (true) value; precision is the degree to which repeated measurements under unchanged conditions show the same results.

with standard procedures (quality intervention) and contractual obligation, etc.]
- Information related to output - will activities lead to output? Are the desired outputs being achieved?
- Information related to challenges, constraints and positive aspects along the way. Challenges, constraints and positive aspects should be overcome, mitigated, and capitalised respectively to ensure successful operation.

The next step is to identify the indicators[12] that provide the required operational information to ensure the effective operation of the programme/projects. Commonly used indicators at the operational level are:

- Process indicators - assist in identifying whether activities are implemented per the plan and set standards.
- Output indicators - indicate how well project outputs are being achieved.

Note:

- Use the process and output indicators of the project for operations-level management. If the required numbers of indicators are not captured in the log frame, it is advisable to develop new indicators for successful operation.

At functional level

We should determine how well support services are enabling the operation. For example:

- How well programme, finance, logistics and HR units/departments work together.
- What are the ongoing needs of the organisation to support the operation?

---

[12] Quantitative ways of measuring and qualitative ways of judging progress toward achieving results.

- Status of the physical assets (stock, vehicle movements & maintenance, working condition of the equipment, etc.) supporting the operation.
- Staff-related matters (knowledge, attitudes, skills, performance, salary, etc.) directly impact the operations.

It is advisable to develop a group of standard indicators to measure the impact of functional-level support in delivering an effective operation.

At performance level

There are two main reasons for measuring our performance:

- Accountability - we need to show those who give us resources and those who benefit from our work that we are using the resources appropriately.
- Lesson learning - by measuring, analysing, and reflecting on our performance, we can learn lessons that will enable us to either change our project plans or change our approach to other projects.

We should periodically judge the overall worth of an endeavour (show accountability) and capture the lessons that assist us to either changing our plans or approaches.

At the very least, we must go through the five international standard criteria to ensure that the programme/project is on track. In other words, the success of the programme/project must be analysed in terms of the following:
- Effectiveness;
- Efficiency;
- relevance/appropriateness;
- impact; and
- sustainability

(for further details, see section 1.7)

Note:

If an NGO engages in similar activities, it is better to develop standard indicators to capture operational, functional and performance information. Then think about the kinds of data to be collected. This process will help to decide where and from whom to collect data, which tools to gather data, and how best to use them to collect the maximum amount of reliable data.

The next step is identifying **what types of data** need to be collected to provide operational, functional and performance information.

Table 4 illustrates how to define data needs. However, it is not a complete picture. It is important to note that data needs will differ for each project. Therefore, special attention is required in each case.

Table 4

Types of information they need	Scope of the Data
Operational information	**Information related to the process** Suggested question: Are the activities implemented per the plan and set standards? - Kind of activities/services - Timing of activities - Progress of the activities - Availability of personnel, service providers, contractors and materials - Use of other resources - Implementation in line with standard procedures - Contractual obligation - Expenses (against budget) - Constraints, challenges, and positive aspects related to the operation - What works well and what does not (related to operation)? - Level of community involvement (physically and financially), community linkages, reaction, and feelings of the end-users, etc.

	Information related to output • Data for output indicators • Beneficiary (who benefited with disaggregated data - when, where and how) • Data related to challenges, constraints, and positive aspects
Functional Information	**Data to be collected to support subsequent analysis** Suggested question: How well do the programme, finance, logistics, and HR units/departments work together? • Analyse any delays in procurement, releasing of funds, the appointment of staff, purchasing • Check any coordination issues that affect the operation • Analyse any issues related to the team spirit that slow down the operation Suggested question: What are the ongoing needs of the organisation to support the operation? • Analyse any additional equipment and resources (human and materials) needed for successful operation • Check if structural rearrangement is needed to support the operation • Analyse if the capacity of the organisation is appropriate to support effective operation Status of the physical assets to support the operation • Check stock details and inventory records • Check that the procurement procedures are aligned with government standards and donor requirements • Analyse if vehicle movements are scheduled appropriately and are taking place as per the schedule (without much deviation) • Check the condition of vehicles, other equipment, maintenance schedule, etc.

	<u>Staff-related matters that directly affect the operation</u> • Check knowledge, attitudes, skills and behaviour of staff are appropriate to the operation • Analyse staff performance and check whether staff adhere to protocols, etc. • Analyse any issues related to staff salary that hamper the operation
Performance Information	• Data to measure the project's/programme's overall success in terms of its effectiveness, efficiency, and appropriateness • Data to measure how the services impact the lives of individual users/clients or target communities (effect of socio-economic factors on services and use) and will the impact be sustainable? • Data that explains the reasons for changes

Having a clear idea about data needs (what types of data are to be collected) helps with decisions about where and from whom to collect data, which tools to use for gathering data, and how best to use them to collect the maximum amount of reliable data.

Step 2: Determining the information and data flow

It is important to note that all the collected data at a certain level needn't be submitted to a higher level. Data must be transformed into information when reporting (see section 1.7 and tables 3 & 4). The most detailed data should be kept at the source, and reporting requirements to higher levels should be kept to a minimum. A major determining factor for this step is the function of the office and the person to whom the data is submitted about the generation and utilisation of information.

The following should be considered while determining the information and data flow:

- Identification of the most appropriate unit and the role of the person to whom data will be submitted for the process.

- Determine what information (operational, functional and performance) will be submitted to whom and decide what types of supportive data must be given.
- Determine how frequently information should be submitted to each level; accordingly, decide how frequently data should be collected.
- Information that is not needed often (e.g., performance) can be submitted quarterly or semi-annually instead of monthly. Therefore, not all data should be generated through the routine data collection system. Data that is not needed frequently can be generated through special studies, surveys, focus group discussions, etc.

An example of a data and information flow diagram is shown in Figure 4

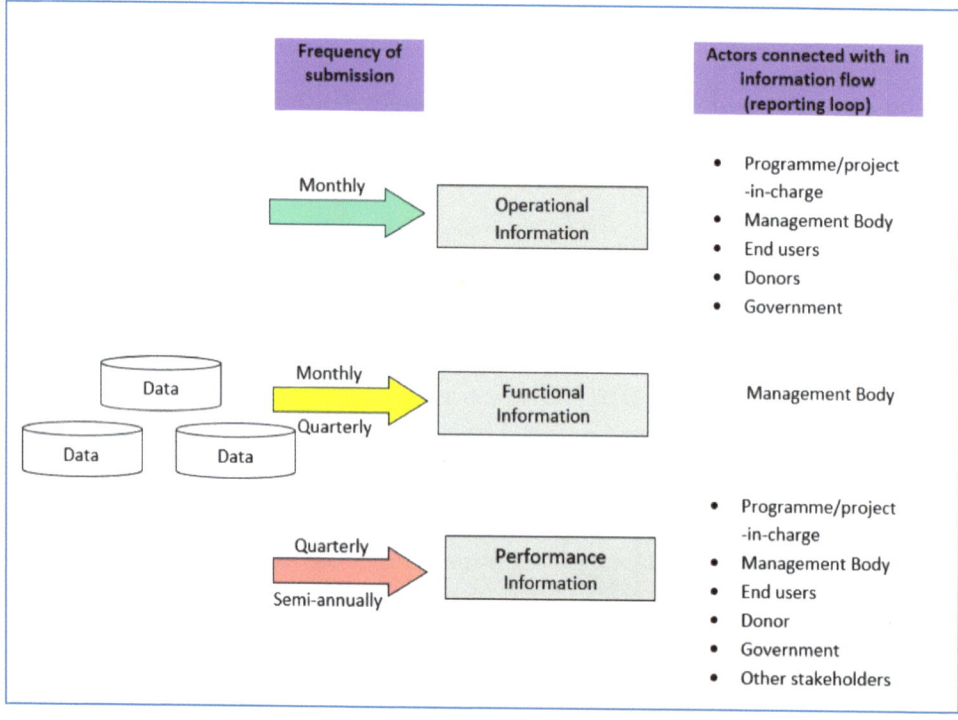

Note: Donors and Government have two types of functions in the social fund: control and strategic (see table 3). For the control function, they need operational information. Therefore, they must be given operational information per the reporting requirement (quarterly or semi-annually).

Step 3: Planning data collection

Once the different types of data that should be collected and the data flow has been identified, the next step is to plan the data collection. The following must be considered when planning data collection:

- What is the required sample[13] size?
- How to collect/gather data?
- How to ensure data quality (see section 1.6)?
- When it should be done (time available to collect data)?
- Who needs to be involved (consider the skills and experience of the staff)?
- How much funding is available to collect data?
- Geographical condition, location, and distance of the respondents
- Literacy level of potential respondents

Based on these conditions, decisions can be made as to what methods and tools will be used for data collection with the support of key players/team/staff. It is advisable to use customised tools as per your need.

Important note:

- The capacity of the staff who will be tasked with collecting data must be taken into consideration while developing tools.
- The most effective data collection and reporting tools are simple and short.

---

[13] Calculate the required sample size for indicators.

- To promote the implementation of systematic data collection and storage (improve consistency), use standard formats[14] that should be accompanied by easy-to-understand explanations and instructions.
- It is advisable to test the forms/questionnaires (used for collecting data) before widespread use by asking a small number of target respondents to respond to the questions. This ensures that the answers given are clear, unambiguous and relevant to the questions.
- If possible, try to verify the accuracy of the data collected using other sources.

Commonly used tools and methods are highlighted in table 5 for collecting data to provide operational, functional and performance information. However, it is not a complete picture. For more details, see annex 1 of this guidebook, which describes data collection tools and techniques.

Table 5

Types of information they need	Scope of the Data	Tools and Methods
	Information related to the process Suggested question: Are the activities implemented per the plan and set standards? • Kind of activities/services • Timing of activities	For the process • Project Implementation Plan[15] • Financial analytical tools

---

[14] Eliminates the incompatibilities and inconsistencies found in different formats/procedures used in different projects and/or at different times and brings compatibility and standardisation of formats/procedures.

[15] Lays out the scheduled activities and sub-activities together with their budget and timeframe on a yearly basis. It is also used to schedule project management-related activities such as monitoring/reviewing/evaluation schedules, reporting deadlines, meeting schedules, logistics plan, finance plan, resource plan, etc. In addition to this, this tool assists in monitoring scheduled elements.

Operational information	<ul><li>Progress of the activities</li><li>Availability of personnel, service providers, contractors and materials</li><li>Use of other resources</li><li>Implemented in line with standard procedure, etc.</li><li>Contractual obligation</li><li>Expenses (against budget)</li><li>Constraints, challenges, and positive aspects related to the operation</li><li>What works well and what does not (related to operation)</li><li>Level of community involvement (physically and financially), community linkages, reaction and feelings of the end users etc.</li></ul> Information related to output<ul><li>Data for output indicators</li><li>Beneficiary (who benefited with disaggregated data, when, where and how)</li><li>Data related to challenges, constraints and positive aspects</li></ul>	Information related to output <ul><li>M&E plan and M&E tool[16], Indicator tracking sheet etc.</li></ul> Beneficiary-related information <ul><li>Specially designed forms or tables as per requirement</li></ul> Information-related challenges, constraints and positive aspects<ul><li>Constraints and lesson learnt logs[17]</li></ul> Commonly used methods Interview, focus group discussion, case study, surveys, observation,

---

[16] It helps monitoring the progress towards the overall and specific objectives as well as the expected results, based on the achievement of indicators specified in the logical framework. In addition, this tool defines a methodology on how these indicators will be recorded (method of data collection, source of information, frequency, and persons in charge of the monitoring).

[17] Assists in capturing constraints, lessons learnt (what works well, what does not).

			gathering data from existing sources [18] etc.
Functional Information		**Data to be collected to support subsequent analysis.** Suggested question: How well do the programme, finance, logistics, and HR units/departments work together? • Analyse any delays in procurement, releasing of funds, appointing staff, purchasing • Check any coordination, issues that affect the operation • Analyse any issues related to the team spirit that slow down the operation Suggested question: what are the ongoing needs of the organisation to support the operation? • Analyse any additional equipment and resources (human and materials) needed for successful operation • Check structural rearrangement is needed to support operation • Analyse if the capacity of the organisation is appropriate to support the operation Status of the physical assets to support the operation	• Checklist • Capacity development plan • Appraisal form • Reporting templates • Inventory record template • Fixed asset register • Stock control sheet • Vehicle running sheet, etc. • Equipment maintenance records Commonly used methods Interview, focus group discussion, surveys, inspection, observation, meetings, document reviews (stock records, procurement procedures, vehicle log, etc.)

---

[18] Detailed data about the local population and their characteristics, such as age, sex, address, family composition, educational level, employment, etc.

	• Check stock details and inventory records • Check that the procurement procedures are aligned with government standards and donor requirement • Analyse if vehicle movements are scheduled appropriately and are taking place as per the schedule (not much deviation) • Check the condition of vehicles, other equipment and maintenance schedule, etc. <u>Staff-related matters that directly affect the operation</u> • Check knowledge, attitudes, skills and behaviour of staff are appropriate for the operation • Analyse the performance of the staff and check whether staff adhere to protocols, etc. • Analyse any issues related to staff salary that hamper the operation	
Performance Information	• Data to measure the programme's overall success in terms of its effectiveness, efficiency, and appropriateness • Data to measure how the services impact on lives of individual users/clients or target communities (effect of socio-economic factors on services and use) and will the impact be sustainable? • Data that explains the reasons for changes	• Questionnaires for interviews. • Pathway/guideline for focus group discussions • Checklist • Case study templates • Mini survey template • M&E plan and M&E tool,

		Indicator tracking sheet, etc. • Financial analytical tools • Survey forms • Reporting templates Commonly used methods Interview, focus group discussion, case study, surveys, observation, desk study etc.

Step 4: Data analysis

Data analysis is the process of converting raw data into useful information. Data analysis involves careful examination of collected data to:

- identify patterns, trends, exceptions and the relationship between different types of data;
- assess performance against targets; and
- forecast anticipated problems/challenges.

This analysis is used to draw meaningful conclusions and solutions.

The way data is processed should be consistent with the objectives for data collection and the plans for data analysis and utilisation.

Phase 1: Organising and preparing the data for analysis (quality control and tabulation)

Quality control

- Check for missing and incomplete records and data and complete them.

- Cross-check the data for accuracy - identify data omissions and apparent errors that might have been made when collecting and recording data. Checking against other records and data sources may help to identify missing or erroneous data. If it is impossible to collect those missing and incorrect data from other sources, collect them again.

For quantitative data[19]

- Extract the data from stored records or forms and tabulate[20] it.
- Break down the data into categories per the need (services by sex, age group, etc.)
- Calculate the indicators such as percentages, ratios, and rates and add them to the tables.
- Draw graphs and charts to visually present key trends or findings.

For qualitative data [21]

- Cluster the information (from interviews, focus group discussions, case studies, and observation field notes) and link to results and indicators. This data may be:
    - facts
    - ideas
    - comments
    - worries
    - suggestions
    - recommendations

Phase 2: Describing the data and producing findings

Remember the following when describing data:

---

[19] It tells you what happened, when, and to whom.
[20] Tabulating data means summarizing the data collected and recorded in various forms into summary tables that can be easily understood and interpreted.
[21] This explains how and why things happen.

- Focus on the objective findings rather than interpreting data with opinion or conclusion.
- Acknowledge how the data is described (e.g., what comparisons or statistical analysis are selected to describe data).
- Acknowledge the assumptions related to the chosen techniques which affect the interpretation.

Method of analysis

It is easy to analyse the data once it has been presented in tables, graphs or charts. Comparison and trend analysis is commonly used to analyse the data in the social fund. Statistical and non-statistical techniques are used for analysing data.

A) Comparison

Table 8 describes how to do a comparison using quantitative and qualitative data.

Table 8

Quantitative Analysis	Qualitative Analysis
	1. Physical progress Is there any variance in objective targets? If so, why? ○ Influence by outside factors? ○ Are any changes in **assumptions/risks** being monitored and identified? If so, why? Does the project/programme need to adapt to these?
Planned versus actual (variances in physical and financial aspects)	Are any functional-level issues hampering the implementation (product and services)? ○ Any delays in procurement, releasing funds, or appointing staff? ○ Any coordination issues, team spirit, etc.? ○ Does anything need to be improved concerning staff knowledge, attitudes, skills, performance, salary, etc.?

- Any ongoing needs of the organisation that affect the implementation (equipment, materials, human resources, structural rearrangement, etc.)
- Is the working relationship among the units or departments suitable?
- Any issues related to the capacity of the organisation?

2. <u>Financial Progress</u>

Is there any variance in the budget? The following questions assist in analysing financial progress:
- Is expenditure broadly in line with the budget?
- Is income broadly in line with the budget?
- Are there any significant variances (temporary[22] or permanent[23])? If so, have they been satisfactorily explained?
- What action is being taken to correct significant variances (e.g., under-spending due to delayed activity implementation?)
- Are there any unbudgeted expenses that may occur during the year?
- How can this be rectified, or do plans need to be updated? (Check the idea, recommendations, or suggestions given by project staff, partners, end-users, stakeholders, etc.)
- What about the quality of financial decisions?

---

[22] Variances caused by a change in the planned timing of an activity (e.g. due to delays or rescheduling) are described as temporary variances because they will most likely work themselves out during the course of the year. These should be monitored and managed internally and are generally less of a concern.

[23] Variances caused by changes in the price or quantity of budgeted items fall into the permanent variances category because once this has happened, there is no going back. The only way to recover the situation is to make an action plan, such as to reduce spending on future items where lines are overspending or increase activity levels where there are savings.

	○ Is any additional information or analysis required to help clarify an issue?
Demographic comparison (e.g., do boys attend school more than girls? Is female participation less than the male?)	Example questions • Why is there a disparity? (Why is the attendance rate for girls less than for boys? Why is the female participation rate lower than the male?) • How can we improve it? (Check the ideas, recommendations or suggestions given by project staff, partners, end-users, stakeholders, etc.) • Is any additional information or analysis required to help clarify an issue?
Geographic comparison (e.g., do people in camp A have better access to services than people in camp B)	• Why? • How can this be rectified? (Check the ideas, recommendations, or suggestions given by project staff, partners, end-users, stakeholders, etc.) • Is any additional information or analysis required to help clarify an issue?
Thematic comparisons (e.g., is shelter design A better than B)	• Why? • Is any additional information or analysis required to help clarify an issue?

B) <u>Trend analysis</u>

The following questions assist in analysing trends.

- ○ Are there any emerging trends/clusters in the data? (quantitative)
  If so, why? (qualitative)
- ○ Are there any similarities in trends from different sets of data? (quantitative)
  If so, why? (qualitative)
- ○ Is the information showing us what we expected to see?
  (the log frame's intended results)
  If not? Why not? Is there anything surprising, and if so, why?

Example

There is a project which focuses on increasing water and sanitation accessibility. In this example, only one indicator is taken for analysis.

Quantitative analysis

To analyse quantitative information, professionals use a traffic light approach that rates data by either i) green for on track against the target, ii) yellow for slightly off track but likely to meet the target, and iii) red for off target and unlikely to meet the target.

Indicators	Target	Actual	Deviation % [% of target]	Explanation of variance
Number of project beneficiaries	2500	2700	8%	
Number of water tanks distributed	200	0	-100%	Delivery of water tanks is hindered due to road access in the rainy season.
Number of community volunteers trained to maintain and supervise drinking water provision	500	400	-20%	Absence of some community volunteers due to harvest season.

In this example, numerical values show what has happened to whom.

> **Qualitative analysis**
>
> Now we must analyse **how and why those things happen**. It can be investigated by asking simple questions.
>
> **Question** - Why are water tanks not being distributed?
>
> **Answer** - Due to the impact of the rainy season, water tanks were not distributed. This is the qualitative information that provides an insightful view of the problem.
>
> **Learning?** - Distribute water tanks before the rainy season.
>
> **Note:** It is easy to capture lessons learned through quantitative and qualitative analyses.

Phase 3: Producing information

As mentioned in section 1.7, a well-defined MIS should provide vital and up-to-date operational, functional and performance information that assists actors in making decisions. Therefore, the findings of the analysis must be presented as information. This session explains how to convert findings into information.

<u>Key steps for producing operational and functional information</u>

> Operational information reveals:
> - how the project functions vis-à-vis outputs, schedules, and the use of resources; and
> - constraints faced, risks and positive changes along the way.

> Functional level information indicates:
> - how well the programme, finance, logistics and HR units/departments work together;
> - ongoing needs of the organisation;

> - status of the physical assets (stock, vehicle movements & maintenance, working condition of the equipment, etc.); and
> - staff-related matters (knowledge, attitudes, skills, performance, salary, etc).

A) List the objective findings related to the operation (activities and outputs).
B) Identify what does not work well at the process and output level (e.g. activities are not implemented as per the schedule and prescribed standards; outputs are not achieved as per the plan, etc.)
C) Point out any unusual trend, if noticed (for example, people in camp A have better access to services than people in camp B).
D) List the causes for variance [24](B and C). It may be constraints, unexpected challenges, a logistics or financial issue, a functional or quality problem, or a combination of these issues.
E) Point out possible solutions to rectify each cause. These can be filtered from opinions, suggestions, recommendations, and facts given by end-users, project teams, stakeholders.)
F) Point out "what works well" and how these achievements can be capitalised on for the successful implementation of the programme/project.

Key steps for producing performance information

> Performance information assists in assessing:
> - how well an organisation is meeting its objectives (effectiveness[25], efficiency[26], relevance[27]);
> - effects of the intervention (impact[28]) on beneficiaries or communities;

---

[24] Suggested question: Why did it happen?
[25] The extent to which the development intervention's objectives were achieved, or are expected to be achieved, taking into account their relative importance.
[26] A measure of how economically resources/inputs (funds, expertise, time, etc.) are converted to results.
[27] The extent to which the objectives of a development intervention are consistent with beneficiaries' requirements, country's needs, global priorities and partners' and donors' policies.
[28] Positive and negative, primary and secondary long-term effects produced by a development intervention, directly or indirectly, intended or unintended.

- continued long-term benefits (sustainability[29]); and
- the reasons for the results (changes).

Consider the followings (keynotes):

- The project goal is a general, often lofty, long-term change. In contrast, outcome refers to the intermediate changes (e.g., improved condition, institutional performance, or behaviour changes) desired among the focus population or their environment.
- Change at objective levels (outcome and impact) happen more slowly. Therefore, frequent data collection at higher levels will not provide much useful information.
- Data that is not needed frequently can be generated through special studies and sample surveys. Widely used key data collection methods are:
    - survey (primarily for collecting quantitative data)
    - desk study (primarily for collecting quantitative data)
    - observation (primarily for collecting qualitative data)
    - case study (primarily for collecting qualitative data)
    - focus group discussion (for collecting both quantitative and qualitative data)
    - interview (for collecting both quantitative and qualitative data)

A) Ensure the programme/project is a good fit for the problem at hand (**relevance**).
B) Decide whether the programme/project is working by measuring the **effectiveness** of the programme/project. Triangulate the finding to ensure the measured changes are due to the programme/project.
C) Check whether the same results (outcome) could be achieved with fewer resources, less money or less time (**efficiency**).

---

[29] The continuation of benefits from a development intervention after major development assistance has been completed. The probability of continued long-term benefits. The resilience to risk of the net benefit flows over time.

D) Use the following calculator[30] to inform evidence-based decision-making about the future of the programme/project.

Relevant/ Appropriate	Effective	Efficient	Conclusion	Decision for next step
√	√	X	Programme is not efficient. The programme is well-targeted and produces the desired results, but the same results could be achieved with fewer resources.	Modify the implementation process to improve efficiency
√	X	√	Programme is not effective. The programme's objectives address an identified need, and it is managed efficiently, but the programme does not deliver the desired results.	Modify or redesign the programme to address the need.
X	√	√	Programme is not appropriate. The programme efficiently achieves the desired outcomes, but there is no longer support/need to act on this issue.	Stop delivery of this programme. It is no longer required.

---

[30] Adapted from *DIY Program Evaluation Kit*.

E) If the programme is relevant, effective, and efficient, then assess the intervention's impact. Identify the long-term effect of the intervention either:
- positive or negative
- intended or not

on individual households, institutions, and the environment caused by a given development activity such as a programme or project.

F) Identify the probability of continued long-term benefits after completing major development assistance.

Note:
- In most cases, evaluating the impact of the project/programme during the programme/project cycle in the social fund is not feasible.
- Mainstreaming is an ultimate test to ensure sustainability - if the end-users are connected with service providers of an existing system (e.g., government system), then there is a high probability of getting continued long-term benefits to end-users after major development assistance has been completed.

Step 5: Ensuring data security

There is a possibility that the stored data (paper record forms or in computerised databases) can be altered, deleted, or lost intentionally or unintentionally. Computers can also be affected by viruses or other forms of corruption. To improve data security, the following actions should be taken:

- Set up permission requirements for using or altering data with different levels of privilege and provide different passwords for each user.
- Make and keep copies of essential data at regular intervals (preferably once a month, both soft and hard copies).
- Install anti-virus software on the computers and update the anti-virus software every week.
- Erect a robust firewall system.
- Back up stored data at regular intervals or when data is modified/updated.

2.3 Stage 3: Dissemination of data and information

Keynotes:

1. We never 'let the data speak for itself as data is an unsystematic fact (raw fact) or detail about something or someone - which may or may not be useful (see section 1.5). Therefore, data must be transformed into useful information (which has some value to users).

2. Information alone cannot be shared as the authenticity (validity) of the information is questionable.

3. To ensure authenticity, both the information and the supporting data must be disseminated

4. Information can be presented manually or via computer technology. Presentation tools include:
    - summary reports
    - leaflets
    - books
    - CD, VCD, DVD

5. Data can be represented visually by:
    - tables
    - graphs
    - pie charts
    - maps
    - photos

6. Information and data can be communicated to other organisations/stakeholders in hard copy, electronically (soft copy), or both, depending on the available communication structure and requirements.

Key steps

A) Consider the following for effective and efficient ways of disseminating information and data:
- To whom (target group) and for what purpose should the information and data be disseminated?
- What should be disseminated? (either operational information or functional information or performance information, or both or all three).
- How often should information and data be disseminated to the different target groups?
- In what form (hard copy or electronically) should information and data be disseminated to each target group?

B) Identify the human, financial and other resources needed to implement the dissemination plan.

C) Prioritise the different modes of data dissemination to be adopted based on need and the availability of resources.

D) Implement the data dissemination activities.

E) Develop and implement a system for monitoring dissemination activities.

ANNEX-1

I - Case study: A detailed descriptive narrative of individuals, communities, organisations, events, programmes or periods. They are particularly useful in evaluating complex situations and exploring qualitative impact.

II - Checklist: A list of items used for validating or inspecting that procedures/steps have been followed or the presence of examined behaviours.

III - Closed-ended (structured) interview: A technique for interviewing that uses carefully organised questions that only allow a limited range of answers, such as "yes/no," or expressed by rating/number on a scale. Replies can easily be numerically coded for statistical analysis.

IV - Community interviews/meetings: A form of public meeting open to all community members. Interaction is between the participants and the interviewer, who presides over the meeting and asks questions following a prepared interview guide.

V - Direct observation: A record of what observers see and hear at a specified site using a detailed observation form. Observation may be of physical surroundings, activities, or processes. Observation is a good technique for collecting data on behaviour patterns and physical conditions.

VI - Focus group discussion: Focused discussion with a small group (usually 8 to 12 people) of participants to record attitudes, perceptions, and beliefs pertinent to the issues being examined. A moderator introduces the topic and uses a prepared interview guide to lead the discussion and elicit discussion, opinions, and reactions.

VII - Key informant interview: An interview with someone with special information about a particular topic. These interviews are generally conducted in an open-ended or semi-structured fashion.

VIII - Laboratory testing: Precise measurement of the specific objective phenomenon, for example, infant weight or water quality test.

IX - Mini-survey: Data collected from interviews with 25 to 50 individuals, usually selected using non-probability sampling techniques. Structured questionnaires with a limited number of closed-ended questions are used to generate quantitative data that can be collected and analysed quickly.

X - Most significant change (MSC): A participatory monitoring technique based on stories about important or significant changes rather than indicators. They give a rich picture of the impact of development work and provide the basis for dialogue over key objectives and the value of development programmes.

XI - Open-ended (semi-structured) interview: A technique of questioning that allows the interviewer to probe and follow up on topics of interest in-depth (rather than just "yes/no" questions).

XII - Participant observation: A technique first used by anthropologists, it requires the researcher to spend considerable time with the group being studied (days) and to interact with them as a participant in their community. This method gathers insights that might otherwise be overlooked, but it is time-consuming.

XIII - Participatory rapid (or rural) appraisal (PRA): This uses community engagement techniques to understand community views on a particular issue. It is usually done quickly and intensively over a two to three-week period. Methods include interviews, focus groups, and community mapping.

XIV - Questionnaire: A data collection instrument containing a set of questions organised systematically, as well as a set of instructions to the enumerator/interviewer about how to ask the questions (typically used in a survey).

XV - Rapid appraisal (or assessment): A quick, cost-effective technique to gather data systematically for decision-making, using qualitative and quantitative methods, such as site visits, observations, and sample surveys. This technique shares many characteristics of participatory appraisal (such as triangulation and multi-disciplinary teams) and recognises that indigenous knowledge is a critical consideration for decision-making.

XVI - Self-administrated survey: Written surveys completed by the respondent, either in a group setting or in a separate location. Respondents must be literate (for example, it can be used to survey teacher opinions).

XVII - Statistical data review: A review of population censuses, research studies, and other sources of statistical data.

XVIII - Survey: Systematic collection of information from a defined population, usually by means of interviews or questionnaires administered to a sample of units in the population (e.g. persons, beneficiaries, and adults).

XIX - Visual techniques: Participants develop maps, diagrams, calendars, timelines, and other visual displays to examine the study topics. Participants can be promoted to construct visual responses to questions posed by the interviewers, for example, by constructing a map of their local area. This technique is especially effective where verbal methods can be problematic due to low literacy or mixed language target populations or in situations where the desired information is not easily expressed in either words or numbers.

XX - Written document review: A review of documents (secondary data) such as project records and reports, administrative databases, training materials, correspondence, legislation, and policy documents.

From: Chaplowe, Scott G.2008." *Monitoring and Evaluation Planning*"." *American Red Cross/CRS M&E Module Series*." American Red Cross and Catholic Relief Services (CRS), Washington, DC and Baltimore, MD.

Reference:

Luc Lecuit, John Elder, Christian Hurtado, François Rantrua, Kamal Siblini, Maurizia Tovo. (1999). *De MIStifying M I S: Guidelines for Management Information Systems in Social Funds.* Retrieved from http://documents.worldbank.org/curated/en/772611468762368827/DeMIStifying-MIS-guidelines-for-management-information-systems-in-social-funds

UNESCO Bangkok (2009). *Developing Management Information Systems for Community Learning Centres: A Guidebook.* Retrieved from https://unesdoc.unesco.org/ark:/48223/pf0000183534?posInSet=1&queryId=79ee821d-b594-403a-a7b4-dd9dfd28ba78

Pathfinder International, *Series-2: Organizational Management, Module-4: Monitoring and Evaluation and Management Information System (MIS.)* Retrieved from http://www2.pathfinder.org/site/DocServer/MIS.complete.pdf

Grosvenor, Public Sector Advisory. *DIY Program Evaluation Kit.* Retrieved from https://www.grosvenor.com.au/resources/diy-program-evaluation-kit/

www.ingramcontent.com/pod-product-compliance
Lightning Source LLC
Chambersburg PA
CBHW040328220526
45473CB00009B/2607